The WORD Works...If You Work IT!
From Poverty to PROMISE!

The
WORD
Works...

If You Work IT!

From Poverty to PROMISE!

Tammy McBride

XULON PRESS

Xulon Press
2301 Lucien Way #415
Maitland, FL 32751
407.339.4217
www.xulonpress.com

Paperback ISBN-13: 978-1-6628-4935-0
Ebook ISBN-13: 978-1-6628-4936-7

TABLE OF CONTENTS

DEDICATION

I dedicate this book to my dear grandmother, Mrs. Catherine (Dozier) Carter. My grandmother lived to be 92-years of age and she made her transition back to Heaven... on my birthday. She was the greatest example for me of someone who committed to live a life that was pleasing to God. Her life's example was the legacy she left to her family. As a child growing up, the one scripture that I often heard my grandmother quote was **Romans 8:31**, *"If God be for us, who can be against us?"* I witnessed what God did for her on her last day on this Earth.

It helped me to believe—God _was_ for her.

FOREWORD

I served as New Members Pastor at our local church for 16 years. One of my primary responsibilities was to orientate joining members into their new church home and to provide a system discovering their God-Given Spiritual Gift; connecting members into areas of ministry according to their gifts and talents. In order to accomplish this, I had to formulate a team of purpose driven; Holy Spirit propelled teachable people to assist with this ministry.

I was fortunate enough to meet Tammy McBride in the Spring of 2011. She volunteered to walk alongside me in the ministry, reaching and teaching new members and ministry servants. Tammy had a heart to serve and did not shy away from the foundational seeds that were sown into her early life, particularly by her loving Grandmother.

The WORD Works...If You Work It! is the background and extension of the harvest of seeds sown in her heart, soul, and spirit. Challenges that could only be altered by sending out The Word of God and knowing it would accomplish all that He desired. As we peek into her journey, we will witness the contagious faith exhibited during trying times; the ups and downs, ins and outs, good and bad, and shaking of life. A vibration so difficult that it led her to open her mouth and speak life to complex situations.

Our words are powerful, they form our life. This book will guide and position you to work the Word. Use the authority that has been given to you by The Father. Speak life to your dying situations!

Dr. Jane Render
Associate Pastor
Word of Faith Family Worship Cathedral and Founder, *"Hear and Be Healed"* Ministry

---

I have served in ministry with Tammy McBride for the last 3 years, and have been tremendously blessed by the magnitude and consistency of her faith.

Tammy has been a faithful and exemplary leader at Word of Faith Family Worship Cathedral for over a decade. She constantly encourages those around her to stand on God's Word and speak His Word aloud to their situation. And watch it work! She frequently shares a new testimony that inspires others, even if it's simply an expression of gratitude for the blessings most people neglect to acknowledge.

The Bible says that *"...faith cometh by hearing and hearing by the word of God"* **(Romans 10:17)**. This book is filled with powerful scripture that inspires faith. And Tammy's conviction about the power of God's Word is contagious.

The Bible also says, *"And they overcame him by...the word of their testimony"* **(Revelation 12:11)**. In this book, Tammy shares meaningful testimonies that have occurred throughout her life to demonstrate the power of faith in God's Word.

Be empowered by God's Word and inspired by the testimonies that comprise this book. Get ready to take the limits off of God. Build your faith, and apply God's Word to every aspect of your life.

Pastor Kristie Brawley
Pastor of Membership Development
Word of Faith Family Worship Cathedral and Author of *"Double Vals: The Keys to Success in College and Life Beyond"* and *"Bridging the Gap: What Teens Wish Their Parents Knew"*

Introduction

Jeremiah 29:11 (NIV)
"For I know the plans I have for you,"
declares the Lord, "plans to prosper you
and not to harm you, plans to give you
hope and a future."

2 Corinthians 1:20 (NKJV)
"For all the promises of God in Him
are "Yes," and in Him "Amen,"
to the glory of God through us."

*P*lain and simple, my sole purpose in writing this book is so that you may be stirred in your spirit to BELIEVE and SPEAK God's Word over your life circumstances, so that "IT" may change those circumstances for the better.

I did that very thing, BELIEVED and SPOKE God's Word... and it changed my life FOREVER! It can do the same for you. Because once you get the revelation and understand how keeping God's Word in your mouth can take you *"into a wealthy place,"* **(Psalm 66:12**), which is where God wants to bless you to be, you will not want to speak anything contrary to His Word again.

At her website https://alexiscarucci.com, Minister Alexis Carucci teaches a lesson about *"God Wants Us to Prosper! – Living the Abundant Life."* She said, "To be blessed means to prosper (to be successful; to thrive) and increase as a result of God's favor upon your life, <u>and it doesn't depend on conditions!</u>"[1]

Scripture **Isaiah 55:11** says, *"So shall my word be that goeth forth out of my mouth: it shall not return unto me void, but it shall accomplish that which I please, and it shall prosper in the thing whereto I sent it."*

BELIEVE and SPEAK God's Word...HE <u>will</u> do the rest!

NOTE: *satan's name is lower cased intentionally. I chose not to give his name importance.

CHAPTER 1

Isn't She Lovely?

Exodus 20:12
"Honour thy father and thy mother:
that thy days may be long
upon the land which the
LORD thy God giveth thee."

y grandmother was the glue that held our family together. She honored God, through Jesus Christ, and trained her family under the precepts of **Proverbs 22:6**, *"Train up a child in the way he should go: and when he is old, he will not depart from it."* She not only set a spiritual foundation for her children, but also for her children's children, to the third and fourth generation. She walked in an intimate relationship with Jesus all of her life. And to this day, I still believe I, and all of my family, continue to walk under the prayers she prayed on our behalf.

My grandmother was born on 3 February 1915. She was the youngest of five children. A short time thereafter, her mother passed. I'm not sure of the circumstances surrounding her death but after she passed, my great-grandfather refused to allow my grandmother and her siblings to be separated. He vowed to keep them with him to raise them up together, and that's what he did.

When my grandmother got married at the age of nineteen, she became pregnant with a total of twelve children. Unfortunately, she said the first four births did not make it to birthing. Granny shared that after the fourth loss; she said she told God that if she lost another baby, it would kill her.

Her fifth pregnancy was the birth of my mother, Lois. After her birth, my grandmother never lost another child. Following the birth of my mom, Granny had seven more children; a surviving total of four girls and four boys.

My grandparents lived less than ten minutes from my parents and it was always a joy to spend time with them. Most times when visiting, Granny would often have some treat waiting for us, either cookies or a cake that she had baked. Growing up, anytime I would visit her, it just felt good just to be in her presence.

Fast forward to 1982, one month after graduating from high school, I left to serve in the United States Air Force. When I would come home on military leave, I would make it a priority to spend time with my grandmother...just the two of us. I loved her German chocolate cake, which she always made from scratch. And I remember during one visit, she and I baked one together. As it was in the oven, it seemed like it was taking a long time to bake so Granny opened the oven door to take a look. When she did, she said, "This cake has fallen!" Then she said, "I don't know how good it's gonna taste." I said, 'Granny, I don't care if it fell. I'm still gonna eat it!' We just laughed.

As I went through my military career, there were numerous times I tried to get stationed close to my home. The closest Air Force base available was at Warner Robins Air Force Base

(AFB) in Georgia. That base was located one hour away from my parents and grandparents.

In 2004, nearing the end of my assignment at Yokota Air Base, Japan, I was due to rotate back to the United States. Once again, I attempted to see if I could get an assignment to Warner Robins AFB. I called the Assignments Office located at Randolph AFB, Texas. Upon calling, I was told there were no slots available at that base for my military rank. At that time, I held the rank of Senior Master Sergeant which was one rank away from the highest rank an Air Force enlisted military member could be promoted to. The highest rank was Chief Master Sergeant. After being informed that no slots were available, I then considered extending my tour in Japan for two additional years because there was no other base I desired to be stationed at stateside except Warner Robins AFB.

But God....He had other plans.

At that time, I was assigned to the Wing Inspector General's office. I worked in the Complaints Department and conducted investigations of complaints. Being assigned there, we (the Inspector General and I) would have to meet with the Wing Commander of the base to brief him on the cases we were investigating and the status of each one. At this particular meeting, as I was approaching the time to transition back to the states, the Wing Commander asked me what base I would like to transition back to. I told him, 'Well, I would like to get stationed at Warner Robins AFB.' Interestingly, the Wing Commander didn't say, "Well, good luck with that," or "Hope it works out for you." Instead he said, "Any particular place you want to work?" When he asked me that question, the hairs on the back of my neck stood up...so to speak.

Two days later, I received a call from the Assignments Office at Randolph AFB informing me that they did, after all, have a position open up for my rank at Warner Robins AFB! That's when I first began to "see" the hand of God move in my life. I believe God used the Inspector General to share with the Wing Commander my desire to be stationed close to my family. Because it was such a quick change of circumstances, I had no doubt that there was a "phone call" made on my behalf. I often think about that time and chuckle. Little did I know as I had gotten in God's way, "trying" in my own power to get assigned to Warner Robins AFB; God already had it in His plans to assign me there. Warner Robins AFB was my last assignment before retiring from the military in August 2005.

When I returned to the states in 2004, my grandmother was in a progressive stage of dementia which advanced to Alzheimer's. Regardless of her condition, I felt blessed that God gave me three wonderful years with her. I helped my mom to care for her, as she became her primary caretaker. My other siblings helped as well, and I personally thought it an honor to care for her at her greatest time of need. As her condition continued to progress, I *cherished* every moment spent with her. I got to bathe her, dress her, feed her, fix her hair, and just sit with her even if we weren't doing anything. I adored my sweet grandmother and I felt so blessed to be there for her. Because Warner Robins AFB was only one hour away from her, I would often go spend time with her during the week as well when I got off work. Back then, a cassette player/recorder still existed, so when I did spend time with her, giving my mother a break, I would press the "Record" button and just let my grandmother talk. There's a saying for loved ones who go through Alzheimer's, "Once an adult, twice a child." Because of the altered state of my grandmother's mind, she would some-times go into her own little world, as I called it, and I wanted to record her talking and laughing. I realized that eventually her life on Earth would come to an end. Granny always had a great sense of humor, even while going through Alzheimer's; she maintained her sense of humor. So, I wanted to be able to hear her voice and her laughter long after she was gone. And to this day, fifteen years later, I'm able to do just that.

And then that time arrived. After retiring from the military, I moved to Atlanta, Georgia in 2006 seeking employment and was able to find a job. It was March 2007, and I was at work when I got a call from my sister. She called to tell me that Granny was non-responsive; so I told her to call for an ambulance. My grandmother never spoke again. She never opened her eyes again. She just lay in bed, looking as if she was just sleeping.

As I said at the beginning, Granny had four girls and four boys. As she went from the hospital, to the hospice center, and finally back home; all of her children had come to visit her by this time except her youngest daughter and youngest son. My mom said Granny had told her she wanted to pass at home, and all of these movements took place as my mom was determined to honor Granny's request and get her home before she passed.

Many years ago, I made a decision to always take my birthday off from work. Even if I was just sitting in my house looking at the four walls, I was <u>not</u> going to be at work. It was 21 March 2007, same day as my birthday, and the hos-pice nurse had come to the house to check on my grand-mother. I remember her telling my mom that she could hear my grandmother's organs beginning to shut down. She told my mother that if there was anyone who wanted to see my grandmother before she passed, they needed to come. I've heard it said that the last of the five senses to leave the body is the sense of hearing (remember that as I continue). So, my mom knew her youngest sister and brother were the last two of Granny's children that had not yet visited her since she became non-responsive.

When my grandfather transitioned in April 1990 from prostate cancer, I was stationed at Osan Air Base, Korea. I remember my sister telling me later that Papa had been in so much pain. I'm not sure if my aunt or uncle felt Granny was suffering and they didn't want to see her that way or it could have been that they just wanted to remember their mother as she was before the dementia/Alzheimer's set in....alive and vibrant. At any rate, my mom called them and told them what the hospice nurse had said. So, they came.

From the day that Granny became non-responsive up until her return back home, for every family member that visited her and talked to her, she just laid in the bed giving no response to their voices. That evening her youngest daughter and son arrived. When they both stood beside Granny's bed and started talking to her, Granny's breathing became so rapid that we all witnessed her chest rising and falling just as rapidly. It...was... AMAZING to see! We all looked at one another wide-eyed, not really knowing what to do, so we just stood there. Then, after a few minutes, she calmed down. This daughter and son continued to talk to her, but she never opened her eyes and she never spoke. They were at her bedside for about an hour or so. When they left, about forty minutes later, we could hear my grandmother's breathing pattern begin to change as she was in the process of taking her last breath. To me, from the moment she became non-responsive up until 21 March (approximately ten days), it was as if she was hanging on to hear the voices of her youngest daughter and son, because she had heard the voices of her other six children, some almost daily.

As Granny was transitioning on my birthday, I was kissing her on her cheek saying, 'Goodbye.' When I tell people that my grandmother passed on my birthday, they respond with condolences. I tell them, 'That's not sadness for me. To me that was favor from God!' I tell them, 'My grandmother stood in the presence of Jesus on MY birthday! That's permanently etched in stone on her grave marker. That will never change!' "Once an adult; twice a child." I never had any children of my own but I remember a time long ago when my mom and I were at Granny's house. One of my five-year old cousins had fallen asleep on the sofa and I got up to move her to the bed. When I scooped her up, I tried to do so as gently as I could so as not to awaken her. Apparently Granny was watching me because as I walked out of the room, I heard her say to my mom, "I think Tammy would make a good momma." As I said, I never had any children, but having had the privilege to help care for my grandmother as she went through Alzheimer's because she was unable to care for herself, I cared for her as if she was my child. To me, she was my baby girl.

Mrs. Catherine (Dozier) Carter
Mother's Day - 2006

GRANDMOTHER
One of Life's Greatest Gifts

CHAPTER 2

A Prophecy &
A Message from God

Jeremiah 37:17
"...Is there any word from the Lord?"

A Prophecy

*I*n September 2005, I traveled to Florida to visit one of my girlfriends. She and I were stationed together at Little Rock AFB, Arkansas where we were both on active duty in the military. By 2005, she too had retired from the military and although we'd kept in touch, we hadn't seen one another for some years.

While there, she and her family were celebrating her step-father's seventy-seventh birthday. Family members attended as well as members from their church. I remember as time passed at this event, my girlfriend, her church Bishop, another gentleman, and I were the only ones inside the event hall at the time. Everyone else had moved outside, enjoying the beautiful day. I remember my girlfriend being seated across from me, the gentleman was seated to my left, and the Bishop was standing up at the food counter. The gentleman seated to my left was eating his food and seemed focused in doing so, because he wasn't engaged in conversing with us. He never even looked up from his plate.

What seemed like all of a sudden, the Bishop asked me, "Tammy, are you a believer?" I said, 'Yes!' I thought to myself, "I can't help but be a believer." As soon as I said, 'Yes!' The gentleman seated to my left, without even looking up from his plate, said, "And she's the chosen one. God's going to use her. It doesn't matter what she's done. It doesn't matter what anyone says. God's going to use her."

The Bishop saw the look on my face and said, "That's nothing to be afraid of." I said, 'I know.' What the gentleman said was just unexpected. And then I thought in my mind, "Wow! God wants to use me. I don't want to mess that up." Oddly enough, the gentleman didn't say anything else to me the remainder of the time we were at the gathering. My girlfriend later told me, "Tammy, that man is a prophet. Everything he's spoken to other people, it's come to pass." I was indeed, in awe!

I have held on to that prophesy to this day. I even give God thanks for choosing me. For all the things that have happened in my life since then, I've seen where and how God has used me. And I live with expectancy, and trust that He will continue to do so because I want to be used by God.

A Message from God

When I retired from the military, unlike other retirees who had done the same, it took me quite a while, about thirteen months, before I found another source of income. On 16 August 2006, I had a job interview with a company I found on the CareerBuilder job search website. Because I do not like to be late and after mapping out the directions to get to the appointment, I decided to leave an hour early in an attempt to be there with time to spare. Directions to the job interview included having to get on Interstates 75/85 and I try to avoid having to get on any Interstate in Atlanta, as much as possible, because driving in the Atlanta traffic while on the Interstate can become challenging.

Although I'd traveled I-75/85 before, somehow, I got turned around and realized I was headed in the wrong direction. Realizing I would be late, I called twice to let it be known, but no one answered the phone. Then, I became more agitated and began having thoughts of just "going back home," or that the job probably "wouldn't be one I'd like." But then, those thoughts were dismissed when suddenly, a calmness came over me and I said to myself, 'Well, all I can do is go to the interview and explain what happened when I get there. They will either go ahead with the interview or tell me it was cancelled because of my lateness.' So I headed to the interview.

When I arrived, the interviewer, Ms. Areka, whom I'd never met, explained the job requirements. It turned out I'd already tried that particular job with another company and found it was not a good fit. The job was training to become a vacuum cleaner salesperson for a specific type high-dollar valued vacuum cleaner. When I had performed a demonstration previously in a potential customer's home, I found conducting the demonstration was quite cumbersome. So, I explained to her that I was not interested in the job. She said she understood.

As I was about to get up to leave, Ms. Areka said, "I have a message for you from God." She said, "I want to be obedient. So, I want to ask if it's okay to share it with you." I told her, 'Yes.' She said, "You don't have to be afraid to ask Him for anything.

11

He already knows. He wants you to ask." She went on to say, "There's some male in your life. Someone you're supposed to be ministering to." She said, "God's going to increase your faith. It's not that you don't already have faith. And He's going to give you a peace like you've never known. But before He can do that, there's some war-faring going on. *satan is trying to control your mind and your thoughts. He also said that there's been some doors closed to you but there's one that's going to open." She ended by saying, "He's also showing me a new car."

Needless to say, with all that she said to me, it was factual. Because what she spoke of was actually the things that were going on in my life at that time. So for me, I received it as God letting me know..."I'm with you." There was a family member that was in between jobs and I let him move in with me. I wasn't as strong in my faith walk then as I am now and so *satan was, in fact, in my head at that time with depressing thoughts because I was so in need of a job and was having a difficult time finding one. It was encouraging to hear of God's plan to increase my faith because at that time, I really needed to hear that. The door that was opened to me was a job with a company that I was hired for shortly thereafter. Ms. Areka mentioning a new car gave me goose bumps because a new car is something I had prayed and asked God for. It wasn't that I needed a new car, because the one I had was fine. But God's Word in **James 4:2** says, *"...ye have not because ye ask not."* That scripture I knew back then so that's what led me to ask. I decided to believe God for my dream car, the Volvo S90 sedan. And I continue to believe Him for it to this day...so much so that, because He is God, I believe for my car to be *paid-in-full* at the time of purchase!

CHAPTER 3

No Matter What...

God Is Always With Us

God Is Always For Us

Psalm 23:4
"Yea, though I walk through the valley
of the shadow of death, I will fear no evil:
for thou art with me..."

*E*ach of the following events that took place in my life are a testament to the "goodness of God" as He showed up:

- To *"work all things to my good"* **(Romans 8:28)**
- To give me *"the desires of my heart"* **(Psalm 37:4 NKJV)**
- To bring to my remembrance that He would *"never leave, nor forsake me"* **(Deuteronomy 31:6 NIV)**

God helped me to realize that no matter how deep the valley; no matter how piercing the darkness...HE is faithful. **Nehemiah 2:18 (NIV)** says, *"I also told them about the gracious hand of my God on me..."* It was these "moves" of the hand of

God in my life that, with each situation, helped to increase my faith in the great *"I AM"* **(Exodus 3:14)**.

As I mentioned in the previous chapter, God sent me a message to say He was going to "increase my faith." From that time forward, I began thanking Him <u>in advance</u> for increased faith. With each of the following situations, God kept His promise and did just that.

A Brand New House

After retiring from the military, I moved from Warner Robins, GA to Atlanta, GA into a three bedroom, two bathroom apartment. I appreciated the fact that my monthly rent was under a thousand dollars considering the area in which I was able to live, Marietta, GA. This area was considered to be one of affluence. I really enjoyed where I lived because it was close to shopping, outdoor ventures, and activities.

After having lived there for almost a year, I received a letter from the Leasing Office informing me that my rent would increase at the time of renewal of my rental contract. That increase would cause my monthly rent to exceed a thousand dollars. That really didn't sit well with me and I remember sitting on my bed and saying, 'God, this is crazy! I'm going to be paying over a thousand dollars a month for a SHELL!' Before the time arrived to renew my contract, I went to the bank and applied for a home loan. The loan was approved and I went house-hunting.

Oddly enough, I never had a desire to live in a subdivision because in too many of the ones that I'd seen, in my opinion, the houses were just too close together. For me, being that close to my neighbor in a subdivision would feel like still living in an apartment. Plus, the house I grew up in as a child sat on four acres of land so I wanted some space between the houses next to me. Inevitably, when a home purchase takes place, it becomes the person's primary residence for life. Realizing this, I just didn't want to have buyer's remorse with where I lived.

Nevertheless, I did go online to look for a house that was in a subdivision and as I did, I connected with a realtor who specialized in selling USED homes. So we began working together to locate a house for me and I told her what I wanted in a house. I wanted trees in the backyard but far away from the house so I wouldn't have to be concerned about a tree falling on the house. I wanted a front porch and for the kitchen sink to have a window above it that would allow me to look out into the backyard. Why? Because those were some of the features that existed with the house that my grandmother lived in. As my realtor was looking for a house with these features, I also looked on my own. I located a house in a newly built subdivision and it was turn-key ready. It had carpet throughout but I let my realtor know I preferred hardwood floors. She told me that if I purchased this house, I could save up some money and later have hardwoods installed. She said her brother-in-law had his own flooring company and she would have him do the work.

She later spoke with the builder of the house and then told me that he wanted me to finance the house through his bank. She said she informed him, "She has a pre-approved loan. And you can't beat the loan she already has." Regardless, she told me, "Well, if you really want this house, you think about it and let me know if you want to finance through his bank." The house was on a corner lot so there was only one house to the left with the street to the right and front side of the house. And the house sat on a decent sized lot.

By the time I made it back to my apartment, I had already made up my mind that I wasn't going to go through re-applying for another loan when I already had a pre-approved loan. I called my realtor and said, 'Let's move on.'

That night I went back online looking at more houses and I found a house that was still in the process of being built. From the photos online I could see that the sod was not yet laid in the yard because I could see that it was still a dirt yard. The dual-garage doors had not been installed. It had a front porch, and I could see tall trees showing in the background. Well, I got so excited that I thought to myself, "I have to go early in the morning to see this house before someone else gets to it!"

When I exited off the website, I noticed I'd received an email from my realtor. In the email she'd sent, she asked me to look at the house that she'd found. She later told me that before she sent me the email, she called her husband into her office and said, "This is it, this is Tammy's house!" When I opened up her email and looked at the house she'd sent me I found...we were looking at the SAME house!

Early that morning, I drove out to see the house, and it was a far distance to drive there. The subdivision was about forty-five minutes away from the apartment. As I continued to drive I was like, 'Okay Lord, how far do I have to drive?' When I finally made it to the subdivision, I immediately understood why the drive was so far out. The builder of this new subdivision built ranch houses on three-quarter to half-acre lots! This meant there was a nice amount of yard between the houses. I realized God sent me far enough outside the city limit to a rural area so that He could give me some land around the house.

The house was so newly built that I got to select the appliances as well as the inside and outside light fixtures. As for the flooring, unbeknownst to me, the builder for this house provided the closing cost. Since there was no closing cost involved, my realtor took that money and surprised me with hardwood floors that she had her brother-in-law install!

My realtor specialized in "used" houses that had been previously lived in. God blessed me with a brand new house! It wasn't even something I was expecting and He gave it to me with a great amount of separation between the houses. Using a self-propelled push lawnmower, it takes me two hours to mow my lawn...I LOVE IT! The house set-up was just like my grandmother's house with a front porch, trees in the backyard, and a window...that's right, located directly above my kitchen sink that allowed me to look into the backyard, just like I wanted. Only God could do that!!

My oldest brother blessed me and took the chairs that used to sit on my grandmother's front porch, gave them a fresh coat of paint, and brought them to me to place them on my front porch. I cannot count the number of times throughout the years, as a family, that we all gathered together on Granny's front porch and sat in those chairs! And now those same chairs sat on my porch. In July 2022, it will be fifteen years that I have lived in this house and to this day, I still walk through it thanking God for blessing me with it and the land that it sits on!

Granny's House of Love

My "Gift" from God

In the Valley with Breast Cancer

In 2012, I had moved on from the "Mom and Pop" business that I'd worked at since 2006. It was a small company and I worked in a one-deep position as the warehouse manager. There was an incident that took place and although the owner used to refer to me as "family," when the incident arose, he chose to ignore it. Not only did he ignore it, but he ignored me. Doing that let me know, it was time to move on, and apparently, I really wasn't family. So I found employment with a company that warehoused food products and to say it was BUSY would truly be an understatement. I was a supervisor on the second shift scheduled to work from 2:30 p.m. to 11:00 p.m. weekdays. Well, that was supposed to be the hours I worked but we actually had to remain at work for as long as it took to ensure all the trucks scheduled for drive-out the next morning were loaded, buttoned-down, and ready to go. There were numerous times we were so busy that I was often leaving the job at 5:00 a.m. heading home while meeting the morning rush hour traffic as those individuals were going to work. That was over twelve hours!

I also was dealing with the challenge of supervising subordinates that were just as exhausted as I was and would often times not <u>care</u> to follow instructions given or fully complete their tasks. That led to coaching sessions, which in my opinion, made matters worse because it led to more rebellion. Management support was not good at all so my peers and I did the best we could under the circumstances. Me personally, I prayed!

While working there, I went to my appointment for my annual mammogram exam. All my previous exams, from the time I began receiving them, were always negative and this included exams performed while I was in the military. This job, without exception, was the most stressful job I'd ever worked; not just for me, but for all who worked there. We were all feeling it. I knew I was stressed and I knew that was not a good thing. So, I remember after the exam was completed, the doctor called me into his office. As soon as he put the x-ray on the screen and said they found cancer; I just smiled because I knew exactly how it came about. I did not cry; I did not fall out or get hysterical; I did not become filled with fear...there was calmness in my spirit that let me know it was time to move on! That very night I went home, sat down at my computer and typed up my resignation letter, because I realized...that job was literally KILLING me!

The doctor explained that the cancer was just developing and was at the stage of calcification, so it was discovered extremely early. I went through the treatment necessary; I had out-patient surgery, went under five days of radiation treatment, and took a pill daily for five years. Having experienced all that stress, I was and still am grateful that by the grace of God, it wasn't worse.

While I actually walked away from this job, I had no Plan B. I walked away because if I had stayed there, I knew the conditions were not going to improve. Management wouldn't care that I'd been diagnosed with cancer. They were about making money for the company. I knew that if I stayed, it was still going to be just as busy. I had no idea how much more working there would affect my body internally, because I knew I would still experience stress. So for that reason, I walked away. Yet, I still had bills to pay and had already been struggling in my finances; still trying to recover from the extended period of time it took for me just to find a job after retiring from the military. I also was, by choice, continuing to help some family members when I could, hoping in spite of that, things would improve. I remember at one time, years ago, asking God, 'If I ever need help, who's going to help me?' God heard and He answered.

God used my oldest brother as His "ram in the thicket." My oldest brother actually paid ALL of my bills to include my mortgage for <u>three</u> months! In addition, after having left that company, I had taken and passed the exam to become a licensed insurance agent. In an effort to create income as an independent agent, I had signed contracts to attend a couple of festival events as a vendor in various areas in and outside of the Atlanta area. As a vendor, once the contract was signed, it was locked in for payment. My brother paid those vendor fees too, and they...were...pricey! My brother helped me and he **never** complained to me about it. He helped me and he **never** said, "One day you need to pay me back." To this day, he has **never** mentioned anything to me about having paid my bills! Even before I went through this valley, my brother had always been a blessing in my life. Having been there for me at my greatest time of need made him an even greater blessing! Even before my diagnosis, I ensured my brother knew, I thank God for him!

In the Midst of Bankruptcy, God Had a Plan

My Bishop at my church often says, "If God told us everything we'd have to go through on Earth, we wouldn't sign up for it." He's right. Many times a person goes through things but often no one may ever know because the person sometimes puts on a façade. But as a believer, when we realize that everything we go through, good or bad, is for <u>God's glory</u>, then we understand nothing is about us, but we trust that God will use what we go through to help someone else. With that understanding, I realize the importance of being transparent as I share having gone through bankruptcy. I pray my testimony will help to encourage others to know that at the lowest point in my life, God came through! Because He did it for me, He can do it for you. Scripture **Romans 2:11** says, *"For there is no respect of persons with God."*

When I retired from the military, I had a hefty savings account with over fourteen thousand dollars in it. I was certain I would find a job quickly without a problem because many employers preferred retired or former military personnel as employees. They took into consideration our discipline, reliability, and sound work ethic. I did get hired for a job on Warner Robins AFB near the flight line, but it was a very brief employment, like, for one week! The very first day I started working there, I could feel an unpleasantness in the atmosphere in that office. In the military, I had worked for a few supervisors who micro-managed the persons they were responsible for. Through observation, on day one, I could sense this supervisor operated with that same management style. I remember him walking me through the shop on the third day and saying to me, "Now, I want you to know, I don't want a "YES" person!" As I failed to read between the lines, I immediately said, 'Oh, you don't have to worry about that!'

On Friday, the ending of my first week working there, the supervisor called me into his office and said they were "moving in a different direction, so we'll have to let you go." Well, I had never been fired before, so I said, 'Okay,' and went back to my desk. About thirty minutes later, I saw one of the females that worked there come out of the supervisor's office and she came to me and said, "He said he'll pay you for the rest of the day."

I told her, 'I want to finish my work!' I had no idea that when a person is fired, they're supposed to gather their belongings and leave immediately! I still laugh about that to this day...duh!

So, I began my job search again. Unfortunately, it wasn't working out finding another job on the base or in the Warner Robins area outside the base, so that's when I moved to Atlanta. Moving there, I still had bills to pay, so I continued to dip into my savings account. One of the bills I had was for a timeshare that I had purchased several years ago when I was stationed at Little Rock AFB, Arkansas. It was by far, one of the most "unwise" decisions I'd ever made that would grow to feel like an "albatross" around my neck. I actually never used the timeshare, yet I had to pay a yearly maintenance fee that started at three-hundred dollars, and with each passing year increased to over nine-hundred dollars by the time I decided to address getting rid of it. I had other bills to pay as well from credit cards, and rent, and a car note, and insurance, and, and, and. So, I thought if I could get rid of the timeshare that I'd been paying on for years, at least I wouldn't have to be concerned about that big bill, because it was my biggest bill, especially since it kept increasing year after year. And there was nothing I could do to prevent it from doing so.

In 2010, I located a financial company that said they provided a service for buying and/or selling timeshares with a processing fee of one-thousand two-hundred fifty dollars. Or I should say I thought I'd found a source. The company was of a reputable name, so I set out to work with the company rep to get rid of the timeshare. We coordinated for almost two months because there were some delays during the process. As time went on, in establishing a rapport with the rep, I let him know that I was a Christian and he, quoting scripture to me, led me to believe he was too. *(Turns out he was a wolf in sheep's clothing)!* I also let him know I would not be paying cash for the processing fee but would be using a credit card. He was okay with that and we moved forward to finalize the contract. When the time came, I gave the rep my credit card information. Two days later after it cleared, I hadn't heard from the company rep, so I called him. When I called the same phone number that I had been calling the entire time period of our communications, I got the following recording, "We're sorry. The number you have dialed has been disconnected or is no longer in service." I was devastated! I'd been talking to this rep for two months and having dialed and got this recording, I realized that although he assured me they were a legitimate company...I had been scammed! I completely lost it! I remember being so distraught, I found myself sitting on my bathroom floor kicking my legs like a two-year old having a temper-tantrum. I called two of my brothers screaming, 'THIS GUY STOLE MY MONEY! HE STOLE MY MONEY!' When I hung up with the one, I called the other. They both did all they could to calm me down, but I remember crying and screaming, **'I'LL NEVER GET RID OF THIS THING!'**

Afterwards, I wrote a letter to the timeshare company to see if there was anything that could be done because I could no longer afford to pay the maintenance fee that kept increasing yearly. Apparently, they were amused and must have thrown the letter in the trash can because they never replied. But they kept mailing me the annual maintenance fee statements.

As the years continued to pass, although I was employed, I was still struggling in my finances. So much so, that one day I decided to total up all my bills. When I did, I realized I had more debt than money! I was just overwhelmed! I felt like I was literally drowning in debt (as I said at the beginning, I'm going to be transparent). Seeing no way out, and having seen the infomercial on TV, I made an appointment with Debt Stoppers to file bankruptcy. **NEVER...IN...MY...LIFE** had I fathomed that I would have to go through bankruptcy, but here I was. I was embarrassed, ashamed, depressed, frustrated, and I remember one day while I was walking in downtown Atlanta headed to the Debt Stoppers office asking myself, 'HOW did I get here?!'

But God had a plan.

When I went in for the initial consultation, the lawyer explained the process. I had heard of Chapter 7 bankruptcy which would wipe out all the debt. But I was told that since I had a job and my military pension, I would have to file Chapter 13 bankruptcy.

Chapter 13 bankruptcy was actually set up to function as a consolidated loan. Filing Chapter 13 bankruptcy allowed me to still pay my creditors and to be honest, I was grateful Chapter 13 existed because my conscious was also bothering me. Not being able to pay back the creditors for the money I had borrowed was a major part of my being depressed. As a Christian, I really wanted to fulfill my obligations from having borrowed money from the creditors. Filing Chapter 13 bankruptcy made it possible for me to do so.

When I went back for the second consultation, I submitted all my documentation. As the lawyer was reviewing it, she said, "You have a timeshare. You wanna keep it?" Before I could even answer, she said, **"Nah, we'll get rid of that!"**

Although I was initially devastated having to file bankruptcy, God *"worked it to my good"* **(Romans 8:28)** because that was the ONLY way I could get rid of that timeshare! And in doing so, it freed me of my ALBATROSS!

CHAPTER 4

Taking God at His Word

Joshua 1:8 (NIV)
"Keep this Book of the Law always on
your lips; meditate on it day and night, so that
you may be careful to do everything written in it.
Then you will be prosperous and successful"

As I have shared, I went through great struggles regarding my finances, but along the way, I was also seeking ways to change my circumstances for the better from a spiritual perspective. I knew that God's Word in **Isaiah 55:11** told me that in speaking His Word, *"He promised that it would... do what He sent it to do."* I read several books that spoke of the benefit in the power of speaking God's Word to my situation and the results that it could create. Specifically, I read a book by Charles Capps titled, *"God's Creative Power for Finances."* Mr. Capps included over twenty-two scriptures in this book and I memorized them to heart. I would speak them sporadically over the years and actually did see some improvement in my finances. Having gone through bankruptcy, which was discharged in 2017, I matured to a place of speaking God's Word consistently in 2019. In doing so, it prospered me from a place of "lack" to a place of "abundance."

At the beginning of January 2019, I was **sick and tired of being sick and tired!!** So I had a talk with God and I told Him, 'Okay God, I'm going to take You at Your Word and start giving Your Word back to You <u>consistently</u>!' I began speaking those twenty-two scriptures daily while in my car, while walking through my house, under my breath at work, or whenever it hit me in my spirit to do so. Months passed and nothing seemed to be changing, but I remained faithful in speaking God's Word aloud consistently.

Then in mid-July 2019, the manifestation began to take place. I received a phone call from my mortgage lender saying they wanted to look at refinancing my mortgage loan to see if they could provide me with a lower interest rate. When the loan officer explained the process and we began, she reviewed all of my debt and she decided to bundle two of my bills into the refinance. Those two bills combined, totaled almost one-thousand dollars and at the completion of the refinance, that money would be coming back to me. Then she asked me if I had a need for a "nest egg" for emergencies. She asked me the amount I desired and told me she would roll that amount into the loan as well. This seemed to be an abnormal prac-tice to me regarding a mortgage loan because these "add-ons" weren't considered with my initial mortgage loan. I was not asked anything about bundling bills or wanting a "nest egg" to deposit in my savings account. So with this refinancing, I received this as favor from God! The process began and by mid-October it was completed.

In the meantime, my sister had shared that she was having car problems that would require repair work that would put a strain on her finances. Since her birthday was coming up in late September and I knew one-thousand dollars would be coming back to me once the refinance was completed, I began looking for a pre-owned car for her. I worked at CarMax and I really wanted to get her a car from there. I know it may seem insignificant, but I wanted the CarMax stamp to appear on the rear of the car, because that's where I worked. And I absolutely love my job! I love what I do. Yet, having gone through a financial valley, I grew in wisdom. I vowed that I would not allow myself to be stretched in my finances ever again. With that decision, taking into consideration my other financial obligations, I realized that the vehicles I found at CarMax would not fit into my newly established financial discipline. So I looked elsewhere.

I searched online and found another car dealership that was, of course, not CarMax. This website had virtual 360-degree photos of the cars on their lot. As I was looking at one particular car in the virtual view, when I saw the backside of this car, there was a stamp on it that read "CARMAX." I was like, 'Okay...that's her car!' I found the car on Thursday and couldn't make it to the dealership until Saturday. On Saturday, we purchased the car, I say we because my oldest brother helped to purchase the car by providing the down payment. He also helped me by driving the car to my sister, as I followed in my car. Talk about an on-time God! Saturday morning my sister was on her way home from having worked the night before and a deer ran out in front of her car. As a result, her car was no longer drivable. So, while God was working things out for me; He was also working things out for my sister!

As I continued to consistently give God's Word back to Him, He continued to show up and show out! At the completion of the refinance, in addition to getting the one-thousand dollars back and depositing money into my savings account, many more blessings came my way. From October through December,

I received FOUR surprise checks in the mail totaling six-thousand five-hundred dollars! The refinancing of my loan was done as a Veteran's Administration (VA) loan. It was explained to me that because I refinanced through a VA loan, there were fees I had been charged that I should not have been charged. As a result, the mortgage lender refunded these monies to me. To me, it was as if these surprise checks were God's way of leaving me *"handfuls of purpose,"* **(Ruth 2:16)** just like Boaz did for Ruth in the Bible. And I give God the glory because since the refinancing of my house, I have NOT been in lack!

At the beginning of January 2019, I barely have TWO nickels to rub together. I made a vow to God that I would activate my FAITH and take Him at His Word. There is <u>no doubt</u> in my mind that because I consistently spoke God's Word back to Him, it turned my financial situation *"for the good!"* **(Romans 8:28, NIV)**. I ended the year of 2019 with more money in my bank account than I'd had in it for a very long time! I was then able to pay my bills as soon as they came in the mail. I was able to be a blessing to someone else without it being a burden. And I give God all the GLORY!!

CHAPTER 5

The Anointing on the Prayer Cloth

Isaiah 10:27
"...the yoke shall be destroyed because
of the anointing."

On Sunday, 18 July 2021, our Bishop announced that Corporate Prayer would be held at the church during the week of August 2nd through August 6th. He said it would begin at 5:00 a.m. on Monday, August 2nd. The Bishop said prayer cloths that he had asked a Woman of God to pray over would be given out. Over twenty years ago, this Woman of God was diagnosed with <u>stage four terminal cancer</u>. With this diagnosis, she activated her faith while going through this sickness. To this day, at 88-years of age, she is *<u>alive and completely healed!</u>* I very much wanted to attend Corporate Prayer to receive a prayer cloth because I believed in the anointing that would be placed on the prayer cloth because of her praying over it. I believed. But I worked on Sunday nights and didn't get off work until 6:00 a.m. Monday morning. I worked the shift alone on Sunday nights and because of that, I pretty much dismissed the thought of being able to attend the service on Monday, August 2nd.

In the meantime in July, at my job, management informed us that because we were not meeting our production numbers, we would have to work additional hours in an effort to do so. At work, we are separated into two production teams. One team works Sunday through Wednesday nights, and the other team works Monday through Thursday nights. Since half the team worked Sunday and Thursday nights, there was only one parts associate working on those nights as well. I was the parts associate that worked alone on Sunday night and there was another parts associate that worked alone on Thursday night. Monday through Wednesday nights, both teams and both parts associates worked, because it was a full house.

Beginning the first week of August, both teams were scheduled to work Sunday through Thursday nights making it a full house, to include both parts associates. With that arrangement, on Sunday night, 1 August, my co-worker and I were both on shift and surprisingly, that night was extremely slow. It was so slow that I left my co-worker in the office and went outside and walked the car lot looking at cars. When I returned to the office, it was still slow. At about 3:50 a.m. the Holy Spirit said to me, "Go ask if you can leave to attend Corporate Prayer." I went to my shift supervisor and explained that my church was starting Corporate Prayer that morning at 5:00 a.m., told him that it was slow in the office, and asked if I could leave to attend. He allowed me to leave since my co-worker was there, so I left.

I made it to the church at 4:45 a.m. that morning and was grateful to be there. I received my prayer cloth and as soon as the service ended and I made it home, I took my prayer cloth and wrote on it, "2 Aug 21/Monday/5 AM/WOF Corporate Prayer – Prayer Cloth for Prosperity." I then put the prayer cloth inside a small plastic bag and placed it inside my wallet next to my money.

My area of need was in my finances and that's why I wanted the prayer cloth. I believed for the anointing it carried. Just like the woman with the issue of blood believed in **Matthew 9:21** *"For she said within herself, If I may but touch His garment, I shall be whole."* That's how I felt about the prayer cloth. I believed for the anointing placed on it for the prosperity of my finances.

Before this same week came to an end, my Operations Manager, who normally would have departed work before I arrived, was still there. He called me into his office and conveyed the company's appreciation for the quality of work I had produced. As a result, he informed me that the company would award a tangible show of that appreciation through a pay raise. It was an unexpected and significant pay raise! Then almost two weeks later, I received a bonus totaling one-thousand dollars! I was informed that I qualified for the bonus via the company's recognition program called "The President's Club." This qualification was due to my accuracy in ordering the correct parts needed to repair the vehicles that would be placed on the car lot for sale. The period of evaluation for this bonus was for the first six months of 2021. I believe these blessings came through the anointing on the prayer cloth! I believed!!

"The Anointing on the Prayer Cloth"

CHAPTER 6

The Grand Finale—
A $35,000 Dollar Blessing!

Ephesians 3:20
"Now unto him that is able to do exceeding abundantly above all that we ask or think, according to the power that worketh in us."

I consider the testimony I am about to share to be the "Grand Finale" in my faith walk with God which led to the writing of this book. For all that I went through in my financial struggles over the years upon retiring from the military; I experienced the faithfulness of God to *honor His Word* as He brought me through every situation. So, in October 2021, it dropped in my spirit to push my faith to the next level and believe God for all of my debt, with the exception of my mortgage, to be paid-in-full <u>before</u> the year 2021 came to an end.

Scripture **Isaiah 55:11**, says, *"So shall my word be that goeth forth out of my mouth; it shall not return unto me void. But it shall accomplish that which I please, and it shall prosper in the thing where to I sent it."*

Scripture **Jeremiah 1:12 (AMP)**, says, *Then the Lord said to me, "You have seen well, for I am [actively]* **watching over My word to fulfill it.***"*

Scripture **Mark 11:23** says, *"For verily I say unto you, That whosoever shall say unto this mountain, Be thou removed, and be thou cast into the sea; and shall not doubt in his heart, but shall believe that those things which he saith shall come to pass; he shall have whatsoever he saith."* In the book mentioned previously, *"God's Creative Power for Finances,"* Mr. Capps says to "Speak to the mountain."[2]

Also, in a book written by Andrew Wommack, *"A Better Way to Pray,"* he said, "The Lord commands us to speak to our problem." He goes on to say, "The Lord told *you* to talk to *it*, not to Him. Whatever *it* is—*speak* to it!"[3] So I started speaking to my mountain and told my mountain what to do.

And scripture **Romans 4:17** says, *"...calleth those things which be not as thou they were."*

At the beginning of October, I made up my mind to go into OVERDRIVE in applying scripture, God's Word, to my financial circumstances. So I took the bills that came in the mail, and for the bills that were automatically debited from my bank account, I wrote them down on a sheet of paper. Then, I laid them out on my bed and every day I spoke to them. I spoke to my "mountain" of debt.

I spoke, declaring over my debt, 'All of my debt is paid-in-full before this year is out!' And I did that every day during my morning prayer. So, October went by and I was like, 'Okay Lord,

You're a God that can do all things. I'm believing that before 2021 is ended, this debt is gone!'

When the month of November arrived, I decided to calculate all of my debt, minus my mortgage payment. I wanted to pay off my credit cards, my car, and the car I was paying on for my sister. I also wanted to help my sister because she was no longer able to work. Yet, she had expressed a desire to get her mortgage paid off and she owed less than ten thousand dollars. Her only income now since she was declared disabled, was a disability check. So, with that as her only income, it would still take her years to pay off her mortgage. I only have one sister and like me, she too from time-to-time experienced struggles with her finances. But because of what I saw her do for our grandmother when she was alive, I committed to helping her whenever I was able to do so.

There was a time when our grandmother was in need, and although sometimes money got tight, as a family, when it came to her, no matter what, we ensured her needs were met. So my parents, my sister, my four brothers, and I, we "circled the wagons," as I called it. And I remember one time, we were putting together the funds to meet a need for Granny. While doing so, I saw my sister set aside paying her bills to give that money to help care for our grandmother. When I saw her do that, I said to myself, "If I ever got a dollar; my sister's got fifty cents." And so that's how I feel about my sister. So I wanted to help her with paying off her mortgage. After I tallied everything up, it totaled $35,000 dollars!

Scripture **Psalm 103:20** says, *"Bless the Lord, ye his angels, that excel in strength, that do his commandments, hearkening unto the voice of his word."* In another book by Charles Capps titled *"Angels"* he says, "Angels are listening." The angels are waiting to hear *"faith-filled words"* come out of our mouth.[4] So during this time when I spoke to my angels, I exercised my authority and commanded, 'Ministering spirits, go to the north, south, east, and west and bring money to me, as men give into my bosom!'

Scripture **Luke 6:38** says, *"Give and it shall be given unto you; good measure, pressed down, and shaken together, and running over, <u>shall men give into your bosom</u>."* The Word says, *"... shall men give into your bosom."* Pastor Wommack said that, "When you ask God for money, He sends it through people!" He goes on to say, "He speaks to individuals and meets your needs through them."[5] Everything we need to prosper on earth, God has already provided; we just have to believe by faith to bring it to pass.

Now it's December, the last month of 2021 and I continue to believe for my debt to be gone. In the past, I've gotten unsecured loans from loan lenders. Their applications offered $3,000, $5,000, or $10,000 dollars. In December, as I was nearing completion to pay back a current loan from one of the lenders, I'd been receiving emails from this same lender saying, "You're doing a great job at making on-time payments on your loan, and we've noticed! Do you need to borrow more money?" Well, I needed $35,000 dollars and I knew this lender <u>only</u> offered up to $10,000 dollars so as they continued to reach out to me via email, I wouldn't even open the email. I just repeatedly swiped left every time to delete the email because talking in my head, I said, "You're only offering me up to $10,000 dollars. I need $35,000 dollars."

Then on Thursday, December 9th, I went to my mailbox and found that in addition to receiving emails from this lender offering me more money, I was now receiving the offer in the mail because there was an envelope in my mailbox from this same lender. I assume the lender was like, "Well, if you're not gonna respond via your email; we'll send the offer to you in the mail." *(I personally believe it was God getting the blessing to me)*. When I removed the envelope from my mailbox and saw that it was from the same lender that had been emailing me, the Holy Spirit said, "Open that envelope." Because the outside of the envelope did not indicate what amount was being offered, the Holy Spirit again said, "Open that envelope." So, I opened the envelope, and sure enough, I was being offered $10,000 dollars. But the flyer inside the envelope was tri-fold, so the top fold showed an offer for $10,000 dollars.

In scripture **Jeremiah 1:12 (ESV)** God says, *"...for I am watching over my word to perform it."* I needed $35,000 dollars to consolidate my debt and then the only monthly payments I would have would be the consolidated debt and my mortgage. My utilities were minimal so my plan was to pay them quarterly. The Holy Spirit said, "Open that envelope." So, I opened the envelope and they approved me for $10,000 dollars, which I thought. But as I continued to unfold the tri-fold flyer, I discovered there was another offer at the bottom of the flyer. The offer at the bottom was for $40,000 DOLLARS!!! Seeing that, I was like, 'Look at GOD!!!' I needed $35,000 dollars!! God *"exceeding abundantly"* **(Ephesians 3:20)**, sent me, through a person, $40,000 dollars!!! Keep in mind, this is an unsecured loan. This does not happen; I received an unsecured loan for $40,000 dollars!! Thirty-five thousand dollars is what I needed.

I got this offer in the mail on Thursday and applied that afternoon. When I woke up Friday morning, I had received an email from the lender saying, "Your loan is approved!" The email stated it would take two to three days before the money would be deposited into my bank account. When I woke up Saturday morning, before I logged into my bank account just to check, I said, 'Lord, let my money be there!' The money was in my bank account Saturday morning!!

In my faith walk, what I know for sure is God wants us to trust Him, to take Him at His WORD and work IT!! And when we work His Word, the angels move! Since 2019, when I made the decision to take God at His Word, I have NOT been in lack! I believed for all of my debt to be paid-in-full before 2021 ended because I just got tired of paying multiple bills every month. I only wanted one bill and my mortgage payment. By faith, God brought it to pass! Scripture **Genesis 18:14** says, *"Is any thing too hard for the LORD?"* For me, God let me know that $35,000 dollars was nothing for Him to handle!! God moved in my finances in a miraculous way!! All of my multiple debts were GONE! And they were gone ***BEFORE*** 2021 came to an end!! TO GOD BE THE GLORY!!!!

CHAPTER 7

The Resources That Helped to Grow My Faith

Romans 10:14
"...and how shall they hear
without a preacher?"

$\mathcal{I}$n addition to the Holy Bible, there were other resources I used to help grow my faith in my area of financial need. I read several books written by people of God who taught on the power behind speaking God's Word to your circumstances. As I was trying to determine how to share these resources with you, it dropped in my spirit to provide THREE specific "nuggets" from each resource to represent the Father, the Son, and the Holy Spirit. My hope is that you will have a desire to add these resources to your library for spiritual growth.

The Law of Confession – Revolutionize Your Life and Rewrite Your Future with the Power of Words – Dr. Bill Winston[6]

1. Dr. Winston talks about four types of confessions. The fourth one that he focuses on is the Law of Confession that brings success in speaking God's will and Word in

faith. It is the one confession that *satan doesn't want Christians to know about because it brings our divine destiny to pass and impacts the world around us with the love and truth and glory of God.

2. You have to make the commitment to stand on God's Word and keep saying it until it is so real in your heart you just can't say anything different. Say it until you fully believe it and are fully persuaded. Then when you speak it, God has to bring it to pass.

3. The only reason the devil still has any influence in the Earth is because the church has not received what God has promised us. God has given us the ability to *"speak those things that be not as though they were"* **(Romans 4:17)** and *"obtain all things that pertain to living a godly life"* **(2 Peter 1:3 NLT)**, but we have not been bold to speak His Word and overcome everything the world does to stop His plan.

Seedtime and Harvest – Charles Capps [7]

1. The Bible method is that you say it the way the Word of God says it. Go to the Word of God, find the promise, and plant that seed. You are seeding for a harvest.

2. When you're talking about the power of words, you're talking about the power of seeds. There is life in God's Word—in the promise itself. It is the life God breathed into it.

3. If you pray one thing and say another, your saying will nullify your praying.

God's Creative Power for Finances – Charles Capps[8]

1. Man is created in the image of God and releases his faith in words. The Word of God, conceived in the human spirit, formed by the tongue, and spoken out of the mouth, is creative power that will work for you.
2. Words are powerful, but God's Word is full of creative power. When you agree with what God has said about you and speak His Word, your circumstances will begin to change and line up with His will for your life.
3. Watch your words—it is vital that you speak only the end result and what you desire. Don't counteract the declarations you have spoken in faith. Manifestations may not come immediately. Hold fast to your confession.

Angels – Charles Capps[9]

1. The angels are governed by the precepts of the Supreme Court of the Universe, which is the Word of God. Their job is to do what God assigns them to do. As you speak God's Word in faith with your own mouth, you commission the angels to move according to that Word.
2. When you begin to confess God's Word in faith and believe it in your heart, God will minister to your needs; the angels will go to work and bring that Word to pass in your life.
3. Your words set the cornerstones of your life. In some instances those words are the very thing that assigns the angels their job. Watch your words! They're powerful!

A Better Way To Pray. If Your Prayer Life is not Working, Consider Changing Directions – Andrew Wommack[10]

1. The spiritual world is the parent force. **(Colossians 1:16; Hebrews 11:3)**. It created everything you see and will still be in existence long after this physical world is gone. **(2 Corinthians 4:18)**. There are spiritual entities— angels, demons, and the Holy Spirit—right where you are! There's a reality within you—your spirit—that you can't come into contact with through your five senses. You just have to believe God's Word, which says, *"When you pray, you receive,"* **(Mark 11:24)**.

2. Faith works by knowledge of the Word. When you ask and believe, the power is instantly released. If you don't see it manifest, it's not God who hasn't given. Either you haven't yet received, or there's a demonic obstacle preventing the manifestation. God is faithful! Believe it and never move off of it!

3. *"My covenant will I not break, nor alter the thing that is gone out of my lips."* **(Psalm 89:34)**. When God gives His Word, He never violates it. He never says something He doesn't mean, and He always means what He says.

CONCLUSION

Isaiah 46:10
"Declaring the end from the beginning..."

Consistently speaking God's Word for the betterment of my financial situation was the <u>one</u> and only change that I made. But that ONE change made all the difference!

Since 2019, I've struggled no more! As I've watched my finances increase from paycheck-to-paycheck and as I've walked to my mailbox only to find junk mail inside instead of bills, like before; I give God all the glory! He manifested the change for me and the manifestation came through His Word! I believed and I spoke! And He delivered me from my valley of debt. The burden was lifted—I no longer have money issues!! And it's the BEST feeling in the world!!

Scripture **Romans 2:11** says, *"For there is no respect of persons with God."* Plain and simple, God has no *"favorites."* He wants all of His children to live a <u>blessed</u> life.

BELIEVE AND SPEAK!!

Endnotes

Introduction

1   Carucci, Alexis, *"God Wants Us to Prosper!—Living the Abundant Life."*
    Source: https://alexiscarucci.com/2020/06/24/god-wants-us-to-prosper/amp/.

Chapter 6 - The Grand Finale - A $35,000 Dollar Blessing!

2   Charles & Annette Capps, *God's Creative Power for Finances,* (Capps Publishing, 2004), England, Arkansas, 26.

3   Wommack, Andrew, *A Better Way to Pray. If Your Prayer Life is not Working, Consider Changing Directions.* (Harrison House Publishers, Shippensburg, Pennsylvania), 2007 by Andrew Wommack Ministries, Inc. Colorado Springs, Colorado, 128.

4   Charles & Annette Capps, *Angels – Knowing Their Purpose, Releasing Their Power*, (Capps Publishing, 1984, 1994), England, Arkansas, 69, 80.

5   Wommack, A Better *Way to Pray, If Your Prayer Life is not Working, Consider Changing Directions, 166.*

Chapter 7 - The Resources That Helped to Grow My Faith

6   Winston, Bill, *The Law of Confession: Revolutionize Your Life and Rewrite Your Future with the Power of Words*

(Harrison House, Tulsa, Oklahoma, 2009), 18, 149, 171-172.

7   Capps, Charles, *Seedtime and Harvest*, (Capps Publishing 1986, 1988), England, Arkansas, 10, 8, 17.

8   Capps, *God's Creative Power for Finances*, 43, 18, 35.

9   Capps, *Angels,* 83, 158, 107.

10 Wommack, *A Better Way to Pray,* If Your Prayer Life is not Working, Consider Changing Directions, 138-139, 176, 125.

CPSIA information can be obtained
at www.ICGtesting.com
Printed in the USA
BVHW060325291022
650416BV00003B/8